FACE
FORWARD

Practices That Will Move You into Your Future

JI NELSON

PRISM
PAGES

Face Forward
© 2021 by Ji Nelson

Printed in the United States of America.

Paperback ISBN: 978-1-7377296-0-0
Hard Cover ISBN: 978-1-7377296-1-7

Library of Congress Control Number: 2021916078

Prism Pages
Highland, California

This is dedicated to my sons
Jiasi Knox & Steel
I love you eternally.

TABLE OF CONTENTS

INTRODUCTION

The words you read in this book will give you practice to help guide you to the future you desire. In the next eight easy-to-ready chapters, you will find simple but powerful and effective ways to build courage, guard your energies, and improve in your own personal development, all while opening yourself to more success and happiness. As you read, do so with confidence that putting these simple practices into place will enhance you in immeasurable ways, and the results will be astounding. Let's begin!

CHAPTER 1:

BRAVERY IS REQUIRED

The truth is you may be doing OK right now. Things in your life may be in a good place, and you may be fairly happy with how things are. It's also possible that you are looking at your life and can see where improvements need to be made. No matter which one of these categories you may fit in, if what you're trying to do doesn't require you to be brave, what you're attempting is probably not going to yield the results you want. Bravery is absolutely required. There's no way around it. While it is not my intention to scare you by saying that, I intend to notify you that greatness comes with unstable, unpredictable moments—the kind of moments where it feels like the floor is evaporating right under your feet, where what was in front of you suddenly disappears, where your mind sinks into questions, doubts, and fears about whether or not you're doing the right thing, or if it's even worth it.

This phase of establishing bravery is also where things and people you felt you could count on may not be as stable or as present as you assumed. You see, true bravery adjusts your variables so that at different points (that are specific to your life's energy and patterns), you have to look within yourself to find strength and the will to continue moving forward; not just simply continuing to move forward, but continuing to move forward without the things that give you comfort and confirmation.

IF WHAT YOU ARE PLANNING TO ACCOMPLISH IS TRULY GREAT, BE PREPARED TO ENCOUNTER INTIMIDATING SITUATIONS. Perhaps it is new people and places. Perhaps there is potentially more money on the table than you are used to dealing with.

This is not the time where you should start second-guessing yourself if those thoughts of doubt start creeping into your mind—just remind yourself that every step toward your future is a show of determination and progress. Little steps are still steps! In all actuality, it's going to take a combination of little steps, big steps, little jumps, and big jumps all along the way. Bravery demands that whenever those steps or jumps are necessary, you take them, even if conditions aren't so comfortable. You will find that once you activate your bravery, you may not be so dependent on all of the external sources of inspiration and comfort you thought you needed. Bravery becomes your best friend—a friend you will undoubtedly need throughout every part of your journey moving forward.

SO HERE ARE A FEW BASIC QUESTIONS YOU MAY BE ASKING:

- ○ WHAT IS BRAVERY?

- ○ HOW CAN I BECOME A BRAVE PERSON?

- ○ HOW LONG WILL IT TAKE FOR ME TO BECOME BRAVE?

LET'S TALK ABOUT IT.

 **BRAVERY IS THIS MAD MIX OF TWO INGREDIENTS: COURAGE AND CONVICTION.**

Courage tells you, "no matter what is happening or will happen, you will keep moving forward, even in the face of fear and doubt." Courage is something you hold tightly until it becomes embedded in your soul. Courage is a power you posses that pushes you through uncertainties. Courage does not mean there is no fear, but it is, most times, activated by fear-inducing thoughts, feelings, or situations. Fear is energy, believe it or not. The more energy fear drains from you, the bigger the energy fear becomes. You know you have courage when you start channeling the energy of fear into energy that causes you to move forward.

I don't want you to think that fear is something you dismiss. It is something you acknowledge and confront. You don't pretend it's not there. You have to know it's there, look at it in the face, and strip it of its power to cripple you.

Conviction says, "you believe deeply in what you're doing and the way it will change the world around you, so it must happen through you." You see, conviction is not simply about believing in "something" but rather believing you are the one this amazing "something" is supposed to happen through. You should believe it so deeply it should be intertwined with how you view and live your life. It should be in the list of truths you live your life by. It is your conviction that will hold your feet to the fire when times of disappointment or discouragement come. On a good or bad day, you'll able to lean on the strength of your conviction when it comes to your success.

○ COURAGE INSPIRES YOU WHILE CONVICTION MAKES YOU RESPONSIBLE.

- COURAGE CHALLENGES YOU WHILE CONVICTION FOCUSES YOU.

- COURAGE WILL STRENGTHEN YOU WHERE CONVICTION GUIDES YOU.

- THEY WORK HAND IN HAND.

See yourself as a brave individual. When you look at yourself, see someone who may feel fear but doesn't stop moving forward. When you look at yourself, see someone who is guided by strong convictions about successful outcomes. You are a winner, and it starts with you seeing yourself as that winner.

Either create or use a phrase that stirs your courage, conviction, and desire to win. Say it whenever you need a boost, and say it as much as you need.

HOW CAN I BECOME A BRAVE PERSON?

This is such an imperative question because, for some people, bravery is a learned behavior. It is a muscle that has to be exercised and flexed to be used whenever and wherever. The way to become a brave person is by finding your **fear-busters**. Yes! **Fear-busters**!

What are **fear-busters**? Let me tell you. **Fear-busters** are small or big things you do to confront small or big fears you may have. It could be anything from public speaking to skydiving. You don't become brave by only thinking about it but by practicing it as well. When you conquer one **fear-buster**, take it up a notch! The goal is to push yourself a bit; **to challenge yourself by going one step past your last fear**. Implementing **fear-busters** will often be the best way to stay in fear-busting shape.

Also, surround yourself with people and things that expect and inspire you to be brave. You have to see bravery, hear it, and feel it to have it at the ready when you need it. The key word here is *become*. There are so many ways to be brave and so many types of bravery that you'll find it to be quite the journey. You'll never run out of ways to be brave. You'll feel the satisfaction of being ready with bravery in some situations, and then you may feel the void when bravery is lacking here and there.

Here is a tip that always helps me. If you are a person who couches or slumps, good sitting or standing posture makes you feel strong and confident. If you are a person who smiles a lot while you look at things other than the person you are talking to, try intentionally making eye contact with whomever you are having a conversation with, realizing that your confidence builds by the second.

Familiarize yourself with your own voice. It sounds crazy, but you'd be surprised at the number of people not used to hearing themselves out loud. Get used to projecting your voice when you speak, always speaking with clarity and a confident tone. Your posture, tone, and voice will not only help you feel confident but will also send a message to whomever you are interacting with that you are ready for the moment.

HOW LONG WILL IT TAKE FOR ME TO BECOME BRAVE?

Here is the simple answer: it is up to you. The moment you decide you need to be brave or braver is the moment you start becoming! It starts with making up your mind. You are brave at the moment you say you are. How brave and what kind of bravery can be determined based on an honest assessment of yourself.

You'll find that not only is bravery required, but it is one of the most important tools in your box!

CHAPTER 2:

WHAT ARE YOU EXPECTING?

know it seems like a simple question, but it's loaded! What are you expecting? You are doing a lot of work, in fact, too much work without being certain of what you expect. What outcomes are you anticipating?

Here is one tip on expectation: sometimes it is **best** to decide what are expecting **before** you start moving because

KNOWING WHAT YOU EXPECT AFFECTS HOW YOU MOVE TOWARD YOUR GOAL.

If you expect to win big before you start moving, you'll move toward that goal with winning confidence. If you expect it to fail, the same applies. You'll start moving toward your goal, but, unfortunately, you place your confidence in your own failure.

What you expect can either assist you or sabotage you. Let me say this clearly: **you decide what you expect**. If all of the variables are working together, then your decision to expect the best worked for you. **Read this slowly**: if the variables are out of whack, but you expected the best in the beginning, you at least have the goal ahead, inspiring you to navigate to your desired outcome, and your decision to expect the best has again worked for you. If you expected to fail, then I have one question . . . **Why**?

Most likely, if you didn't expect to come out on top, it's because you know you need some work in certain areas. Working on those areas will change your expectation, especially when you know you are prepared (and informed) before you go into a situation. I hope you caught that.

PREPARATION AFFECTS EXPECTATION.

WHILE PREPARATION IS POWERFUL, EXPECTATION IS A SUPER POWER! Do I need to explain? No problem. Let's say you prepared all you could, but it's still seemingly not enough; however, you still expect a favorable outcome; your great expectation can somehow shift things around! It's what I call the "Power of Positive." Sometimes the energy of positivity and expecting the best can make up for what you may have lacked in preparation. **Expectation uses and creates tangible and intangible energy**. This is why deciding your expectations are important.

However, I would never encourage you to not use your own intelligence. There are some things that just won't work, no matter how positive you are, and you know it beforehand. In situations like this, it is always good to keep your feet planted in reality. Again, ask yourself:

"What is stripping me of my confidence in this present moment?"

○ IS MY CREDIT NOT WHERE IT SHOULD BE?

○ ARE MY FINANCES NOT THE WAY THEY SHOULD BE?

○ ARE MY CONNECTIONS AND RELATIONSHIPS WHAT THEY SHOULD BE?

Honestly answering those questions and fixing them will give you a reason to expect the best outcome should you ever revisit that situation or any similar one that didn't work out.

Take a moment and think about some of the areas in your life where you expect the best.

Now take a moment and think about some of the areas in your life where you may not expect the best.

Work on those areas. Make them as strong as the areas where you have great confidence. Do it so that you can **expect** to win in every area of your life!

IF YOU AREN'T DOING IT ALREADY, START EXPECTING TO:

- ○ WIN!

- ○ SUCCEED!

- ○ ACCOMPLISH!

- ○ UPGRADE!

IF YOU EXPECT TO INCREASE IN WEALTH AND KNOWLEDGE AT EVERY TURN, YOU WILL MOVE LIKE IT! LET'S MOVE!

CHAPTER 3:

WHAT YOU
HAVE IS NEEDED

There are roughly 7.7 billion people in the world! Hear me loud and clear:

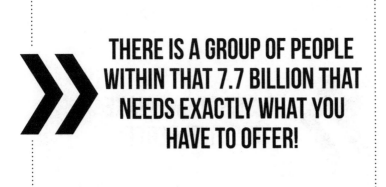

THERE IS A GROUP OF PEOPLE WITHIN THAT 7.7 BILLION THAT NEEDS EXACTLY WHAT YOU HAVE TO OFFER!

What is your thing? What is your business, talent, or service to the community? Whatever it is, there is someone, somewhere, who is looking for it. Remember that part of the conviction we discussed earlier had to do with realizing there is a need for what you offer, and it has to come through you. In a world that seems unbelievably saturated with the same things, offers, ideas, you have to have confidence that what you offer is needed. That is in part because of the unique quality it takes to come through the portals of your mind, thought, creativity, and hands. **What you do is already special, but when it comes through you, it is extraordinarily special**.

This is why you have to make sure what you do has your prints all over it—your style, flavor, personality, and rhythm. The truth is someone, somewhere, is doing the same thing you are doing. In fact, many people may be doing it, but no one can do it quite like you. It stands out because your prints are different. It would do you some good to observe how your style makes what you do different, and then project that difference!

DISTINCTIONS MAKE THE DIFFERENCE!

Always remember that. Details aren't necessarily distinctions, and it is possible for details to be common and uniform. But if something is distinct, that means it would not be usual but something unique that sets it apart from the others.

- ○ IT DOES SOMETHING DIFFERENT THAN THE REST.

- ○ IT FEELS DIFFERENT THAN THE REST.

- ○ IT FITS DIFFERENT THAN THE REST.

- ○ IT SMELLS DIFFERENT THAN THE REST.

- ○ IT TASTES DIFFERENT FROM THE REST.

TAKE A MOMENT AND ASK YOURSELF THESE QUESTIONS:

- ○ ARE PEOPLE SEEING YOUR PRINT/DISTINCTIONS?

- ○ ARE YOU MAXIMIZING YOUR DISTINCTIONS?

- ○ IF NOT, HOW CAN YOU START?

Remember that your customers, clients, patients, investors, mentees, supporters, and so forth are somewhere within the 7.7 billion people in this world, and they need what **you** have.

Do your best to identify them. Acknowledge them, communicate with them, and inspire them by serving them what they need from you.

Did you get that? If you did, don't forget it!

**SERVE THEM WHAT
THEY NEED FROM YOU.**

CHAPTER 4:

EYES AHEAD

yes ahead. Focused. Locked in. The things in front of you are things you need to see. You need to see them to connect with or avoid them, use them or go around them. I'm going to say something now that may seem so ridiculously simple, but it is crucial:

LOOKING BACKWARD AT THE MOMENT YOU SHOULD BE LOOKING FORWARD COULD COST YOU YOUR FUTURE!

Some people look back and fall into a trance, staring at past success. Some people look back and fall into a trance, glaring at past failures. The problem isn't that you are staring at it; the problem is that what you are staring at is behind you.

When you can't keep your eyes ahead, you either:

1. STOP MOVING FORWARD;

or

2. YOU KEEP MOVING FORWARD WHILE LOOKING BACKWARD AND RISK STUMBLING/FALLING OVER SOMETHING AHEAD OF YOU.

Learning from the past is necessary, but being in the present while caught in a past loop could be detrimental to your future. One thing I say out loud frequently is this statement:

EVERYTHING I NEED IS RIGHT IN FRONT OF ME.

When I look forward, I'm expecting and looking for everything I need to be in front of me and not behind. That's right. I am expecting the people, resources, and information I need to be somewhere in my line of sight when I need them. This is not to say that things in the past cannot be beneficial and used again in the future. Some things/people make progress with you, and that's how you know they belong in your journey forward and upwards. They move ahead with you, out of your yesterday, through your today, and into your tomorrow. What hasn't moved with you most likely shouldn't continue to go with you.

Keeping your eyes ahead keeps your mind, spirit, and body ready for your future success. Make no mistake about it, **it takes discipline**! There will be times when you have to fight the urge to look back. You'll have to fight the urge to turn around and re-live that pain or pleasure. One of the scriptures from the Bible I use to remind me of the need to stay future-focused is:

"NO ONE, HAVING PUT HIS HAND TO THE PLOW, AND LOOKING BACK, IS FIT FOR THE KINGDOM OF GOD."

-Luke 9:62

There is a kingdom in front of you. There is a royal future awaiting you. But you can forfeit it all by looking back if you aren't careful. When you keep your eyes future-focused, you train them to weed out anything that doesn't look like the success you envision. Here is the beautiful thing to remember: as long as you keeping waking to see another tomorrow, there is a daily chance to renew your commitment to the future and a healthy outlook toward it.

Take a look around you right now. Everything you see around you can change for the better! Even if it's already great, it can get even better! As you keep your eyes forward, allow your vision to grow and expand. Don't forget, what you need for the future is right in front of you.

Do this:

Write down the positive things you see in your future when you look ahead. Write down the things you believe you'll have, and go into detail with what you see. If you take a look at what you wrote, I'm sure it is so amazing you can see you should allow nothing to interfere with your forward progress in achieving and obtaining those goals. Keep your eyes on it. Another Bible scripture says:

"WHERE THERE IS NO VISION, THE PEOPLE PERISH."

-Proverbs 29:18

Put differently, you can lose if you don't keep the vision in front of you.

Here is a helpful hint for those times when you can't see so well what's ahead.

SAY WHAT YOU WANT TO SEE UNTIL YOU CAN SEE IT AGAIN.

That's right! When your eyes can't see it, your mind will create a visual based on what you hear yourself saying.

If you need to get your phone and record a voice memo of you describing something you see for yourself in the future, play it whenever you need to.

Use your ears (what you hear) **to keep your eyes focused**!

By applying this practice, you can encourage and inspire yourself to stay future-focused and eyes forward.

CHAPTER 5:

THE COMPARISON TRAP

The comparison trap is a dangerous loop to get caught in. One of the strongest impediments to making forward progress is always comparing yourself to others!

 YOUR LIFE HAS ITS OWN TIMING AND ENERGY. FOCUS ON THAT.

You have to trust that things will happen for you when they are supposed to. Put your work in, put your time in, and expect the best outcomes for you. When you compare your success to others, it may inspire you to do more; that's true. But if you aren't careful, you'll find yourself comparing what you have to what someone else has, or what you have done to what someone else has done, and **you may find yourself**

chasing something that was never meant for you at all. No one wants to waste that kind of time.

Learn from others, be inspired by others, and help others. Just make sure you stay away from the destructive, useless competitions that can form in your head. Instead, reserve that energy for your mind, creativity, and stamina. Comparing is not the problem, but getting trapped in destructive comparisons is a problem indeed. Here is what I mean:

HEALTHY COMPARISONS:

INSPIRE

ENCOURAGE

EXPAND

DESTRUCTIVE COMPARISONS:

INTIMIDATE

DISCOURAGE

DRAIN

Have you ever caught yourself staring at something and had to force yourself to break your gaze? If you catch yourself looking at something that generates the wrong thoughts and feelings, break your gaze! The same goes for your hearing. If you hear something that brings you down, find a way to disconnect from what you're hearing. Find something inspiring to you. It should be something that generates feelings of happiness and confidence that you can do whatever you put your mind to do.

Remember that all of the great things in your life are all on schedule. That's right; you have your schedule for your greatness. Everyone else has a timing and rhythm of their own. As they follow theirs, make sure you follow yours.

BELIEVE ME WHEN I TELL YOU THE GOOD THINGS THAT HAPPEN FOR YOU WILL BE SPECIFIC TO YOU.

Here is something you can do! Set goals for yourself so that if you feel the need to compare, you can compare your success this month to your success last month, or this week's gains to last week's gains. Compare today's growth to yesterday's growth. As you follow these tips, you'll find you have more space in your head and emotions for creative ideas and meaningful wins.

CHAPTER 6:

PROTECT YOUR PROPELLERS

IS THERE SOMETHING OR SOMEONE SPECIAL THAT SEEMS TO BE A NATURAL GO-TO WHEN INSPIRING CREATIVITY AND PLANS? If you happen to be like me, you know there are certain things or perhaps certain people that put you in a space to be your best. Whatever it is that puts you in the right space to dream, plan, and create is what I call a **propeller**. It is an engine that moves you forward into the direction you want to go. As you identify your propellers, make sure you protect them!

ASK YOURSELF:

○ IS THERE SOMEONE I TALK TO WHO ALWAYS INSPIRES ME TO DO BETTER?

○ IS THERE A CERTAIN PLACE THAT ALWAYS MAKES ME FEEL CREATIVE OR PRODUCTIVE?

○ IS THERE A CERTAIN KIND OF MUSIC OR MOVIE THAT HELPS ME FOCUS?

If you were able to answer any of these questions, your answer is one of your propellers.

You protect your propellers by keeping them in a special place where you realize they are not common and should not be treated that way. Most of your interaction with your propellers should be because they inspire you to do or be whatever it is you want. Let me give you an example. There are certain places I go when I want to write. I don't go there just to hang out frequently. Whenever I go to these places, it is purposefully to write and nothing else. When you use your propellers frivolously for every single thing, you wear them out, and when you need them, there's a possibility that they will be overused if not tapped out completely.

Keep the special things and places special. There are certain songs I only listen to when I need some energy and momentum to do something I may not feel like doing. And because I know the purpose I have assigned to those songs, hearing them reminds me of my responsibility to get it done. I don't play them every day. It may be weeks or months before I play them because I only play them when I need that kind of boost. Those songs are my propellers.

There are certain people I talk to when I plan, strategize, or come up with ideas. I don't talk to these people about every single thing, I only talk to them in certain spaces because of the good energy they help me generate. I am very careful not to get into arguments or tension-filled conversations with these people over random things because these special people are my propellers.

These are just some simple examples of my propellers. I have many more! There are scriptures, poems, pictures, quotes, candles, incense, and other things I turn on when I need forward motion. The key is every propeller is specific, special, and not something I view or use casually.

If your propeller is a business that provides an environment for you to tap into your genius, make sure you support that business. Buy that cup of coffee, scone, or sandwich that you will become known for as you create your multi-million dollar dream.

IF YOUR PROPELLER IS A PERSON, BUY THEM LUNCH OR GIVE THE OCCASIONAL GIFT TO SHOW APPRECIATION. YOU MAY HAVE ONE, OR LIKE ME, YOU MAY HAVE A FEW. THE NUMBER OF PROPELLERS DOESN'T MATTER. WHAT IS IMPORTANT IS THAT YOU SEE THEM AS PART OF YOUR STORY AND PROTECT THEM AS THEY HELP PUSH YOU INTO YOUR PURPOSE.

CHAPTER 7:

THE MIRROR

A long your face-forward journey, there should come a time when you look at yourself in the mirror to self-check. Yes! A private time where you can make an honest, intimate assessment of yourself. How have you grown in your process? How are you the same? Should you be the same, and if not, what changes do you need to make? Here's the deal: the amazing things you set out to do should challenge and change you for the better! Along the way, you should see how the process polishes you.

You should expect to see some areas of growth that are pleasant to acknowledge, and you should also expect to see some areas where you will have to admit you need work, even if it's not easy or pleasant. This is necessary because as you grow and create a bigger better business, idea, or product, you also want to make sure your personal development is where it should be. If you do too much of something and need to do it less or not at all, the mirror is the place to admit that. Conversely, if you're not doing something or not doing enough of something, the mirror is the place were you admit that.

LEARN TO TRUST THE MIRROR! SEE IT AS AN HONEST, SAFE PLACE. YOUR MIRROR IS THERE SO YOU CAN SEE, TALK, CORRECT, AND ENCOURAGE YOURSELF. IT IS THERE FOR YOU TO MEASURE HOW FAR YOU HAVE COME, WHERE YOU ARE NOW, AND HOW FAR YOU NEED TO GO.

In my experience, there is only enough room in your mirror for you. There is no room in your mirror for everyone else's expectations or opinions. Sometimes we tend to see ourselves through other people's eyes, but your mirror is a portal where your eyes are the only eyes that matter.

Remember this: the mirror is not there for you to beat yourself up. It is not there for you to tear yourself down. The purpose of the mirror is for positive polish and growth. Even in times when you are disappointed in yourself, approach your reflection with respect, honesty, encouragement, and a charge to keep going. That person in the mirror is the closest person in the world to you. Make sure that the two of you are friends!

CHAPTER 8:

GIVE AND BE GRATEFUL

These two will offer you one of the most powerful combinations you will ever experience in your quest to move forward. Giving and gratitude, when you put them together, have a way of starting a **cycle of good**. Your gifts and gratitude go much further than you would ever realize, and they return to you from places you may not be expecting. I'll share a short prayer with you I pray quite often:

 LORD, GIVE ME FAVOR IN PLACES I HAVEN'T BEEN, WITH PEOPLE I HAVEN'T MET YET.

Giving and gratitude opens the door for this prayer to be answered.

Whether it's giving money, time, energy, or wisdom, make sure you're always giving!

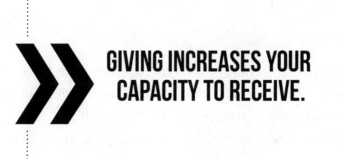

GIVING INCREASES YOUR CAPACITY TO RECEIVE.

That is so powerful! If you want to receive more, give more! It is a principle that works whenever you use it, no matter who uses it.

Here is a scripture that makes it crystal clear:

"GIVE, AND YOU WILL RECEIVE.
YOUR GIFT WILL RETURN TO
YOU IN FULL—PRESSED DOWN,
SHAKEN TOGETHER TO MAKE
ROOM FOR MORE, RUNNING
OVER, AND POURED INTO YOUR
LAP. THE AMOUNT YOU GIVE WILL
DETERMINE THE AMOUNT
YOU GET BACK."

-Luke 6:38

Couple your giving with gratitude. Make it a habit to be grateful for everything! Gratitude is not simply a feeling but an acknowledgment; yes, an acknowledgment. Gratitude is the power and willingness to find the good in bad situations and acknowledge it wherever it may be. This might sound quite pedestrian, but if you make a habit of finding good, good will make a habit of finding you.

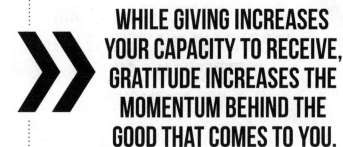

WHILE GIVING INCREASES YOUR CAPACITY TO RECEIVE, GRATITUDE INCREASES THE MOMENTUM BEHIND THE GOOD THAT COMES TO YOU.

Consider this:

"YOU MUST EACH DECIDE IN YOUR HEART HOW MUCH TO GIVE. AND DON'T GIVE RELUCTANTLY OR IN RESPONSE TO PRESSURE. 'FOR GOD LOVES A PERSON WHO GIVES CHEERFULLY.' AND GOD WILL GENEROUSLY PROVIDE ALL YOU NEED. THEN YOU WILL ALWAYS HAVE EVERYTHING YOU NEED AND PLENTY LEFT OVER TO SHARE WITH OTHERS."

-2 Corinthians 9:7–9

That, my friends, is what we should all want: to always have everything we need and plenty left over to share with others.

I call principles like this one a blank check because it's completely up to you how much you fill in the blanks! How much you give of yourself is up to you, and that determines how much you get in return. The good part about this is you always get back more than you give out. Even a little good goes a long way, and imagine how far much giving and gratitude will take you. You literally cannot lose with these two!

SO NOW GO!

ACHIEVE, OBTAIN, EXECUTE,

AND WIN BIG!

FACE FORWARD JOURNAL

This journal will help you to map out a 52 Monday through Friday week journey into your amazing future. Here is how it works:

- THE FIRST THING YOU WILL DO IS DECIDE WHAT PROGRESS YOU EXPECT TO HAVE MADE BY THE END OF THE WEEK.

- THE SECOND STEP IS TO LIST THINGS THAT NEED TO BE DONE.

- THIRDLY, EACH DAY LIST YOUR ACCOMPLISHMENTS AND PROGRESS TOWARD YOUR WEEKLY AND DAILY GOALS.

- FOURTH, WRITE DOWN ANYTHING THAT YOU HAVE LEARNED ABOUT YOURSELF IN THE PROCESS.

- AND LASTLY, GRADE YOUR PROGRESS AND PERFORMANCE FOR THE WEEK BY LOOKING AT THE EXPECTATIONS YOU DECIDED AT THE BEGINNING OF THE WEEK.

As you journal, you will get to know yourself better and become more efficient and productive in meeting your goals.

Now let's get started.

WEEK 1

Challenge yourself by going one step past your last fear.

What I expect to have accomplished by the end of this week:

_____

_____

_____

_____

_____

Monday:_____

Tuesday: _____

Wednesday:_____

Thursday: _____

Friday: _____

What have you learned about yourself?_____

_____

_____

What have you learned about what you are doing? _____

_____

_____

Did you meet your goals and expectations? _____

_____

_____

If your answer is yes, how so? If your answer is no, why not?

_____

_____

Was your week an overall success? Check one.

Yes, it was! _____ I'll do better next week _____

WEEK 2

Knowing what you expect affects HOW you move toward your goal. You decide what you expect.

What I expect to have accomplished by the end of this week:

_____

_____

_____

_____

_____

Monday:_____

Tuesday: _____

Wednesday:_____

Thursday: _____

Friday: _____

What have you learned about yourself?_____

_____

_____

What have you learned about what you are doing? _____

_____

_____

Did you meet your goals and expectations? _____

_____

_____

If your answer is yes, how so? If your answer is no, why not?

_____

_____

Was your week an overall success? Check one.

Yes, it was! _____ I'll do better next week _____

WEEK 3

Preparation affects expectation·

What I expect to have accomplished by the end of this week:

_____

_____

_____

_____

_____

Monday:_____

Tuesday: _____

Wednesday:_____

Thursday: _____

Friday: _____

What have you learned about yourself?_____

_____

_____

What have you learned about what you are doing? _____

_____

_____

Did you meet your goals and expectations? _____

_____

_____

If your answer is yes, how so? If your answer is no, why not?

_____

_____

Was your week an overall success? Check one.

Yes, it was! _____ I'll do better next week _____

_____
_____
_____
_____
_____
_____
_____
_____
_____
_____
_____
_____
_____
_____
_____
_____
_____
_____
_____
_____
_____
_____
_____
_____
_____
_____
_____
_____

WEEK 4

While preparation is powerful,

expectation is a super power!

What I expect to have accomplished by the end of this week:

_____

_____

_____

_____

_____

Monday:_____

Tuesday: _____

Wednesday:_____

Thursday: _____

Friday: _____

What have you learned about yourself?_____

_____

_____

What have you learned about what you are doing? _____

_____

_____

Did you meet your goals and expectations? _____

_____

_____

If your answer is yes, how so? If your answer is no, why not?

_____

_____

Was your week an overall success? Check one.

Yes, it was! _____ I'll do better next week _____

WEEK 5

What you do is already special, but when it comes through you, it is extraordinarily special·

What I expect to have accomplished by the end of this week:

_____

_____

_____

_____

_____

Monday:_____

Tuesday: _____

Wednesday:_____

Thursday: _____

Friday: _____

What have you learned about yourself?_____

_____

_____

What have you learned about what you are doing? _____

_____

_____

Did you meet your goals and expectations? _____

_____

_____

If your answer is yes, how so? If your answer is no, why not?

_____

_____

Was your week an overall success? Check one.

Yes, it was! _____ I'll do better next week _____

WEEK 6

Everything you need is right
in front of you.

What I expect to have accomplished by the end of this week:

_____

_____

_____

_____

_____

Monday:_____

Tuesday: _____

Wednesday:_____

Thursday: _____

Friday: _____

What have you learned about yourself?_____

_____

_____

What have you learned about what you are doing? _____

_____

_____

Did you meet your goals and expectations? _____

_____

_____

If your answer is yes, how so? If your answer is no, why not?

_____

_____

Was your week an overall success? Check one.

Yes, it was! _____ I'll do better next week _____

WEEK 7

Your life has its own timing and energy.
Focus on that.

What I expect to have accomplished by the end of this week:

_____

_____

_____

_____

_____

Monday:_____

Tuesday: _____

Wednesday:_____

Thursday: _____

Friday: _____

What have you learned about yourself?_____

_____

_____

What have you learned about what you are doing? _____

_____

_____

Did you meet your goals and expectations? _____

_____

_____

If your answer is yes, how so? If your answer is no, why not?

_____

_____

Was your week an overall success? Check one.

Yes, it was! _____ I'll do better next week _____

WEEK 8

The good things that happen FOR you
will be specific TO you.

What I expect to have accomplished by the end of this week:

_____

_____

_____

_____

_____

Monday:_____

Tuesday: _____

Wednesday:_____

Thursday: _____

Friday: _____

What have you learned about yourself?_____

_____

What have you learned about what you are doing? _____

_____

Did you meet your goals and expectations? _____

_____

If your answer is yes, how so? If your answer is no, why not?

_____

Was your week an overall success? Check one.
Yes, it was! _____ I'll do better next week _____

81

WEEK 9

The things and people that put you in the right space to dream, plan, and create are your propellers. Make sure you protect them.

What I expect to have accomplished by the end of this week:

_____

_____

_____

_____

Monday:_____

Tuesday: _____

Wednesday:_____

Thursday: _____

Friday: _____

What have you learned about yourself?_____

_____

_____

What have you learned about what you are doing? _____

_____

_____

Did you meet your goals and expectations? _____

_____

_____

If your answer is yes, how so? If your answer is no, why not?

_____

_____

Was your week an overall success? Check one.

Yes, it was! _____ I'll do better next week _____

_____
_____
_____
_____
_____
_____
_____
_____
_____
_____
_____
_____
_____
_____
_____
_____
_____
_____
_____
_____
_____
_____
_____
_____
_____
_____
_____
_____
_____
_____

WEEK 10

Your mirror is there so you can see, talk, correct, and encourage yourself.

What I expect to have accomplished by the end of this week:

_____

_____

_____

_____

_____

Monday:_____

Tuesday: _____

Wednesday:_____

Thursday: _____

Friday: _____

What have you learned about yourself?_____

_____

_____

What have you learned about what you are doing? _____

_____

_____

Did you meet your goals and expectations? _____

_____

_____

If your answer is yes, how so? If your answer is no, why not?

_____

_____

Was your week an overall success? Check one.

Yes, it was! _____ I'll do better next week _____

WEEK 11

*Your mirror is a portal where your eyes
are the only eyes that matter.*

What I expect to have accomplished by the end of this week:

_____

_____

_____

_____

_____

Monday:_____

Tuesday: _____

Wednesday:_____

Thursday: _____

Friday: _____

What have you learned about yourself?_____

_____

_____

What have you learned about what you are doing? _____

_____

_____

Did you meet your goals and expectations? _____

_____

_____

If your answer is yes, how so? If your answer is no, why not?

_____

_____

Was your week an overall success? Check one.
Yes, it was! _____ I'll do better next week _____

_____
_____
_____
_____
_____
_____
_____
_____
_____
_____
_____
_____
_____
_____
_____
_____
_____
_____
_____
_____
_____
_____
_____
_____
_____
_____
_____

WEEK 12

Giving and gratitude, when you put them together, have a way of starting a cycle of good.

What I expect to have accomplished by the end of this week:

_____

_____

_____

_____

_____

Monday:_____

Tuesday: _____

Wednesday:_____

Thursday: _____

Friday: _____

What have you learned about yourself?_____

_____

_____

What have you learned about what you are doing? _____

_____

_____

Did you meet your goals and expectations? _____

_____

_____

If your answer is yes, how so? If your answer is no, why not?

_____

_____

Was your week an overall success? Check one.

Yes, it was! _____ I'll do better next week _____

_____

_____

_____

_____

_____

_____

_____

_____

_____

_____

_____

_____

_____

_____

_____

_____

_____

_____

_____

_____

_____

_____

_____

_____

_____

_____

_____

_____

_____

_____

_____

_____

WEEK 13

Lord, give me favor in places I haven't been, with people I haven't met yet.

What I expect to have accomplished by the end of this week:

_____

_____

_____

_____

_____

Monday:_____

Tuesday: _____

Wednesday:_____

Thursday: _____

Friday: _____

What have you learned about yourself?_____

_____

_____

What have you learned about what you are doing? _____

_____

_____

Did you meet your goals and expectations? _____

_____

_____

If your answer is yes, how so? If your answer is no, why not?

_____

_____

Was your week an overall success? Check one.

Yes, it was! _____ I'll do better next week _____

WEEK 14

Giving increases your capacity to receive.

What I expect to have accomplished by the end of this week:

_____

_____

_____

_____

_____

Monday:_____

Tuesday: _____

Wednesday:_____

Thursday: _____

Friday: _____

What have you learned about yourself?_____

_____

What have you learned about what you are doing? _____

_____

Did you meet your goals and expectations? _____

_____

If your answer is yes, how so? If your answer is no, why not?

_____

Was your week an overall success? Check one.

Yes, it was! _____ I'll do better next week _____

WEEK 15

Luke 6:38: "Give, and you will receive. Your gift will return to you in full—pressed down, shaken together to make room for more, running over, and poured into your lap. The amount you give will determine the amount you get back."

What I expect to have accomplished by the end of this week:

_____
_____
_____
_____
_____

Monday:_____
Tuesday: _____
Wednesday:_____
Thursday: _____
Friday: _____
What have you learned about yourself?_____
_____
_____

What have you learned about what you are doing? _____
_____
_____

Did you meet your goals and expectations? _____
_____
_____

If your answer is yes, how so? If your answer is no, why not?
_____
_____

Was your week an overall success? Check one.
Yes, it was! _____ I'll do better next week _____

WEEK 16

While giving increases your capacity to receive, gratitude increases the momentum behind the good that comes to you.

What I expect to have accomplished by the end of this week:

_____

_____

_____

_____

Monday:_____

Tuesday: _____

Wednesday:_____

Thursday: _____

Friday: _____

What have you learned about yourself?_____

_____

_____

What have you learned about what you are doing? _____

_____

_____

Did you meet your goals and expectations? _____

_____

_____

If your answer is yes, how so? If your answer is no, why not?

_____

_____

Was your week an overall success? Check one.

Yes, it was! _____ I'll do better next week _____

WEEK 17

What I expect to have accomplished by the end of this week:
_____
_____
_____

Monday:_____
Tuesday: _____
Wednesday:_____
Thursday: _____
Friday: _____
What have you learned about yourself?_____
_____
_____

What have you learned about what you are doing? _____
_____
_____

Did you meet your goals and expectations? _____
_____
_____

If your answer is yes, how so? If your answer is no, why not?
_____
_____

Was your week an overall success? Check one.
Yes, it was! _____ I'll do better next week _____

WEEK 18

Expect Cycles of Good!

What I expect to have accomplished by the end of this week:

_____

_____

_____

_____

_____

Monday:_____

Tuesday: _____

Wednesday:_____

Thursday: _____

Friday: _____

What have you learned about yourself?_____

_____

_____

What have you learned about what you are doing? _____

_____

_____

Did you meet your goals and expectations? _____

_____

_____

If your answer is yes, how so? If your answer is no, why not?

_____

_____

Was your week an overall success? Check one.

Yes, it was! _____ I'll do better next week _____

WEEK 19

Keep the special things and places special.

What I expect to have accomplished by the end of this week:

_____

_____

_____

_____

_____

Monday:_____

Tuesday: _____

Wednesday:_____

Thursday: _____

Friday: _____

What have you learned about yourself?_____

_____

_____

What have you learned about what you are doing? _____

_____

_____

Did you meet your goals and expectations? _____

_____

_____

If your answer is yes, how so? If your answer is no, why not?

_____

_____

Was your week an overall success? Check one.

Yes, it was! _____ I'll do better next week _____

WEEK 20

Learn from others, be inspired by others, and help others.

What I expect to have accomplished by the end of this week:

_____

_____

_____

_____

_____

Monday:_____

Tuesday: _____

Wednesday:_____

Thursday: _____

Friday: _____

What have you learned about yourself?_____

_____

What have you learned about what you are doing? _____

_____

Did you meet your goals and expectations? _____

_____

If your answer is yes, how so? If your answer is no, why not?

_____

Was your week an overall success? Check one.

Yes, it was! _____ I'll do better next week _____

WEEK 21

Distinctions make the difference!

What I expect to have accomplished by the end of this week:

_____

_____

_____

_____

_____

Monday:_____

Tuesday: _____

Wednesday:_____

Thursday: _____

Friday: _____

What have you learned about yourself?_____

_____

_____

What have you learned about what you are doing? _____

_____

_____

Did you meet your goals and expectations? _____

_____

_____

If your answer is yes, how so? If your answer is no, why not?

_____

_____

Was your week an overall success? Check one.

Yes, it was! _____ I'll do better next week _____

WEEK 22

Expect to increase in wealth and
knowledge at every turn.

What I expect to have accomplished by the end of this week:

_____

_____

_____

_____

_____

Monday:_____

Tuesday: _____

Wednesday:_____

Thursday: _____

Friday: _____

What have you learned about yourself?_____

_____

_____

What have you learned about what you are doing? _____

_____

_____

Did you meet your goals and expectations? _____

_____

_____

If your answer is yes, how so? If your answer is no, why not?

_____

_____

Was your week an overall success? Check one.

Yes, it was! _____ I'll do better next week _____

WEEK 23

Expectation uses and creates tangible and intangible energy.

What I expect to have accomplished by the end of this week:

_____

_____

_____

_____

_____

Monday:_____

Tuesday: _____

Wednesday:_____

Thursday: _____

Friday: _____

What have you learned about yourself?_____

_____

_____

What have you learned about what you are doing? _____

_____

_____

Did you meet your goals and expectations? _____

_____

_____

If your answer is yes, how so? If your answer is no, why not?

_____

_____

Was your week an overall success? Check one.

Yes, it was! _____ I'll do better next week _____

WEEK 24

You don't become brave by only thinking about it but by practicing it as well.

What I expect to have accomplished by the end of this week:

_____
_____
_____
_____
_____

Monday:_____
Tuesday: _____
Wednesday:_____
Thursday: _____
Friday: _____
What have you learned about yourself?_____
_____
_____

What have you learned about what you are doing? _____
_____
_____

Did you meet your goals and expectations? _____
_____
_____

If your answer is yes, how so? If your answer is no, why not?
_____
_____

Was your week an overall success? Check one.
Yes, it was! _____ I'll do better next week _____

_____
_____
_____
_____
_____
_____
_____
_____
_____
_____
_____
_____
_____
_____
_____
_____
_____
_____
_____
_____
_____
_____
_____
_____
_____
_____
_____
_____
_____

WEEK 25

Surround yourself with people and things
that expect and inspire you to be brave.

What I expect to have accomplished by the end of this week:

_____

_____

_____

_____

Monday:_____

Tuesday: _____

Wednesday:_____

Thursday: _____

Friday: _____

What have you learned about yourself?_____

_____

What have you learned about what you are doing? _____

_____

Did you meet your goals and expectations? _____

_____

If your answer is yes, how so? If your answer is no, why not?

_____

_____

Was your week an overall success? Check one.

Yes, it was! _____ I'll do better next week _____

WEEK 26

Make moves like you area big deal and

you expect to win big·

What I expect to have accomplished by the end of this week:

_____

_____

_____

_____

_____

Monday:_____

Tuesday: _____

Wednesday:_____

Thursday: _____

Friday: _____

What have you learned about yourself?_____

_____

What have you learned about what you are doing? _____

_____

Did you meet your goals and expectations? _____

_____

If your answer is yes, how so? If your answer is no, why not?

_____

Was your week an overall success? Check one.

Yes, it was! _____ I'll do better next week _____

WEEK 27

Find the good in everything that you possibly can this week.

What I expect to have accomplished by the end of this week:

_____

_____

_____

_____

_____

Monday:_____

Tuesday: _____

Wednesday:_____

Thursday: _____

Friday: _____

What have you learned about yourself?_____

_____

What have you learned about what you are doing? _____

_____

Did you meet your goals and expectations? _____

_____

If your answer is yes, how so? If your answer is no, why not?

_____

Was your week an overall success? Check one.

Yes, it was! _____ I'll do better next week _____

WEEK 28

Celebrate! You're making progress.

What I expect to have accomplished by the end of this week:

_____

_____

_____

_____

_____

Monday:_____

Tuesday: _____

Wednesday:_____

Thursday: _____

Friday: _____

What have you learned about yourself?_____

_____

_____

What have you learned about what you are doing? _____

_____

_____

Did you meet your goals and expectations? _____

_____

_____

If your answer is yes, how so? If your answer is no, why not?

_____

_____

Was your week an overall success? Check one.

Yes, it was! _____ I'll do better next week _____

WEEK 29

Courage and conviction. Believe that you are the one for the job and have no fear.

What I expect to have accomplished by the end of this week:

_____

_____

_____

_____

_____

Monday:_____

Tuesday: _____

Wednesday:_____

Thursday: _____

Friday: _____

What have you learned about yourself?_____

_____

_____

What have you learned about what you are doing? _____

_____

_____

Did you meet your goals and expectations? _____

_____

_____

If your answer is yes, how so? If your answer is no, why not?

_____

_____

Was your week an overall success? Check one.

Yes, it was! _____ I'll do better next week _____

WEEK 30

Make sure you take breathers, breaks,
and moments to refresh.

What I expect to have accomplished by the end of this week:

_____
_____
_____
_____
_____

Monday:_____
Tuesday: _____
Wednesday:_____
Thursday: _____
Friday: _____
What have you learned about yourself?_____
_____
_____

What have you learned about what you are doing? _____
_____
_____

Did you meet your goals and expectations? _____
_____
_____

If your answer is yes, how so? If your answer is no, why not?
_____
_____

Was your week an overall success? Check one.
Yes, it was! _____ I'll do better next week _____

WEEK 31

Pace yourself.

What I expect to have accomplished by the end of this week:

_____

_____

_____

_____

_____

Monday:_____

Tuesday: _____

Wednesday:_____

Thursday: _____

Friday: _____

What have you learned about yourself?_____

_____

_____

What have you learned about what you are doing? _____

_____

_____

Did you meet your goals and expectations? _____

_____

_____

If your answer is yes, how so? If your answer is no, why not?

_____

_____

Was your week an overall success? Check one.

Yes, it was! _____ I'll do better next week _____

WEEK 32

There are 7.7 billion people in the world. Someone is looking for exactly what you have to offer.

What I expect to have accomplished by the end of this week:

_____

_____

_____

_____

_____

Monday:_____

Tuesday: _____

Wednesday:_____

Thursday: _____

Friday: _____

What have you learned about yourself?_____

_____

_____

What have you learned about what you are doing? _____

_____

_____

Did you meet your goals and expectations? _____

_____

_____

If your answer is yes, how so? If your answer is no, why not?

_____

_____

Was your week an overall success? Check one.

Yes, it was! _____ I'll do better next week _____

WEEK 33

Don't forget that your happiness is important.

What I expect to have accomplished by the end of this week:

_____

_____

_____

_____

_____

Monday:_____

Tuesday: _____

Wednesday:_____

Thursday: _____

Friday: _____

What have you learned about yourself?_____

_____

_____

What have you learned about what you are doing? _____

_____

_____

Did you meet your goals and expectations? _____

_____

_____

If your answer is yes, how so? If your answer is no, why not?

_____

_____

Was your week an overall success? Check one.

Yes, it was! _____ I'll do better next week _____

WEEK 34

Tap into what inspires you this week.

What I expect to have accomplished by the end of this week:

_____

_____

_____

_____

_____

Monday:_____

Tuesday: _____

Wednesday:_____

Thursday: _____

Friday: _____

What have you learned about yourself?_____

_____

_____

What have you learned about what you are doing? _____

_____

_____

Did you meet your goals and expectations? _____

_____

_____

If your answer is yes, how so? If your answer is no, why not?

_____

_____

Was your week an overall success? Check one.

Yes, it was! _____ I'll do better next week _____

WEEK 35

Be open to change. Sometimes ideas get even better when you start the work.

What I expect to have accomplished by the end of this week:

_____

_____

_____

_____

_____

Monday:_____

Tuesday: _____

Wednesday:_____

Thursday: _____

Friday: _____

What have you learned about yourself?_____

_____

_____

What have you learned about what you are doing? _____

_____

_____

Did you meet your goals and expectations? _____

_____

_____

If your answer is yes, how so? If your answer is no, why not?

_____

_____

Was your week an overall success? Check one.

Yes, it was! _____ I'll do better next week _____

WEEK 36

Take the time to make sure your prints
are all over your project!

What I expect to have accomplished by the end of this week:

_____

_____

_____

_____

_____

Monday:_____

Tuesday: _____

Wednesday:_____

Thursday: _____

Friday: _____

What have you learned about yourself?_____

_____

What have you learned about what you are doing? _____

_____

Did you meet your goals and expectations? _____

_____

If your answer is yes, how so? If your answer is no, why not?

_____

Was your week an overall success? Check one.

Yes, it was! _____ I'll do better next week _____

WEEK 37

Win! Succeed! Accomplish! Upgrade!

What I expect to have accomplished by the end of this week:

_____

_____

_____

_____

_____

Monday:_____

Tuesday: _____

Wednesday:_____

Thursday: _____

Friday: _____

What have you learned about yourself?_____

_____

_____

What have you learned about what you are doing? _____

_____

_____

Did you meet your goals and expectations? _____

_____

_____

If your answer is yes, how so? If your answer is no, why not?

_____

_____

Was your week an overall success? Check one.

Yes, it was! _____ I'll do better next week _____

WEEK 38

Don't forget to pray when you need help.

What I expect to have accomplished by the end of this week:

_____

_____

_____

_____

_____

Monday:_____

Tuesday: _____

Wednesday:_____

Thursday: _____

Friday: _____

What have you learned about yourself?_____

_____

_____

What have you learned about what you are doing? _____

_____

_____

Did you meet your goals and expectations? _____

_____

_____

If your answer is yes, how so? If your answer is no, why not?

_____

_____

Was your week an overall success? Check one.

Yes, it was! _____ I'll do better next week _____

_____

_____

_____

_____

_____

_____

_____

_____

_____

_____

_____

_____

_____

_____

_____

_____

_____

_____

_____

_____

_____

_____

_____

_____

_____

_____

_____

_____

WEEK 39

*Eyes Forward! Eyes Forward! Let the
past stay where it is.*

What I expect to have accomplished by the end of this week:

_____

_____

_____

_____

_____

Monday:_____

Tuesday: _____

Wednesday:_____

Thursday: _____

Friday: _____

What have you learned about yourself?_____

_____

_____

What have you learned about what you are doing? _____

_____

_____

Did you meet your goals and expectations? _____

_____

_____

If your answer is yes, how so? If your answer is no, why not?

_____

_____

Was your week an overall success? Check one.

Yes, it was! _____ I'll do better next week _____

WEEK 40

*Confidence is key. Work on the areas
where you need more of it.*

What I expect to have accomplished by the end of this week:

_____
_____
_____
_____
_____

Monday:_____
Tuesday: _____
Wednesday:_____
Thursday: _____
Friday: _____
What have you learned about yourself?_____
_____
_____

What have you learned about what you are doing? _____
_____
_____

Did you meet your goals and expectations? _____
_____
_____

If your answer is yes, how so? If your answer is no, why not?
_____
_____

Was your week an overall success? Check one.
Yes, it was! _____ I'll do better next week _____

WEEK 41

*Be honest with yourself· It's hard to fix
what you won't admit·*

What I expect to have accomplished by the end of this week:

_____

_____

_____

_____

_____

Monday:_____

Tuesday: _____

Wednesday:_____

Thursday: _____

Friday: _____

What have you learned about yourself?_____

_____

_____

What have you learned about what you are doing? _____

_____

_____

Did you meet your goals and expectations? _____

_____

_____

If your answer is yes, how so? If your answer is no, why not?

_____

_____

Was your week an overall success? Check one.

Yes, it was! _____ I'll do better next week _____

WEEK 42

Can you imagine all the amazing ways that you are going to change things around you?

What I expect to have accomplished by the end of this week:

_____

_____

_____

_____

_____

Monday:_____

Tuesday: _____

Wednesday:_____

Thursday: _____

Friday: _____

What have you learned about yourself?_____

_____

_____

What have you learned about what you are doing? _____

_____

_____

Did you meet your goals and expectations? _____

_____

_____

If your answer is yes, how so? If your answer is no, why not?

_____

_____

Was your week an overall success? Check one.

Yes, it was! _____ I'll do better next week _____

WEEK 43

Make helping people a priority.

What I expect to have accomplished by the end of this week:

_____

_____

_____

_____

_____

Monday:_____

Tuesday: _____

Wednesday:_____

Thursday: _____

Friday: _____

What have you learned about yourself?_____

_____

_____

What have you learned about what you are doing? _____

_____

_____

Did you meet your goals and expectations? _____

_____

_____

If your answer is yes, how so? If your answer is no, why not?

_____

_____

Was your week an overall success? Check one.

Yes, it was! _____ I'll do better next week _____

WEEK 44

Remember, keep your vision in front of you.
Write it. Draw it. Record it. Speak it.

What I expect to have accomplished by the end of this week:

_____
_____
_____
_____
_____

Monday:_____
Tuesday: _____
Wednesday:_____
Thursday: _____
Friday: _____
What have you learned about yourself?_____
_____

What have you learned about what you are doing? _____
_____

Did you meet your goals and expectations? _____
_____

If your answer is yes, how so? If your answer is no, why not?
_____

Was your week an overall success? Check one.
Yes, it was! _____ I'll do better next week _____

WEEK 45

Always take a moment to see the horizon!

What I expect to have accomplished by the end of this week:

_____

_____

_____

_____

_____

Monday:_____

Tuesday: _____

Wednesday:_____

Thursday: _____

Friday: _____

What have you learned about yourself?_____

_____

_____

What have you learned about what you are doing? _____

_____

_____

Did you meet your goals and expectations? _____

_____

_____

If your answer is yes, how so? If your answer is no, why not?

_____

_____

Was your week an overall success? Check one.

Yes, it was! _____ I'll do better next week _____

WEEK 46

Things connected to you grow when you do.
Always grow.

What I expect to have accomplished by the end of this week:

_____

_____

_____

_____

_____

Monday:_____

Tuesday: _____

Wednesday:_____

Thursday: _____

Friday: _____

What have you learned about yourself?_____

_____

_____

What have you learned about what you are doing? _____

_____

_____

Did you meet your goals and expectations? _____

_____

_____

If your answer is yes, how so? If your answer is no, why not?

_____

_____

Was your week an overall success? Check one.

Yes, it was! _____ I'll do better next week _____

WEEK 47

This week say "thank you" every chance you get.
You'll be surprised how much good it will bring you.

What I expect to have accomplished by the end of this week:

_____

_____

_____

_____

Monday:_____

Tuesday: _____

Wednesday:_____

Thursday: _____

Friday: _____

What have you learned about yourself?_____

_____

_____

What have you learned about what you are doing? _____

_____

_____

Did you meet your goals and expectations? _____

_____

_____

If your answer is yes, how so? If your answer is no, why not?

_____

_____

Was your week an overall success? Check one.

Yes, it was! _____ I'll do better next week _____

WEEK 48

While you imagine what you want in your mind, feel it in your body. Transport yourself there. Make it as real of an experience as you can and then say, "It's mine."

What I expect to have accomplished by the end of this week:

_____

_____

_____

_____

_____

Monday:_____

Tuesday: _____

Wednesday:_____

Thursday: _____

Friday: _____

What have you learned about yourself?_____

_____

_____

What have you learned about what you are doing? _____

_____

_____

Did you meet your goals and expectations? _____

_____

_____

If your answer is yes, how so? If your answer is no, why not?

_____

_____

Was your week an overall success? Check one.

Yes, it was! _____ I'll do better next week _____

WEEK 49

Mistakes happen along the way. Learn from them and realize that the mess-ups are not the destination. Keep going!

What I expect to have accomplished by the end of this week:

_____

_____

_____

_____

_____

Monday:_____

Tuesday: _____

Wednesday:_____

Thursday: _____

Friday: _____

What have you learned about yourself?_____

_____

_____

What have you learned about what you are doing? _____

_____

_____

Did you meet your goals and expectations? _____

_____

_____

If your answer is yes, how so? If your answer is no, why not?

_____

_____

Was your week an overall success? Check one.

Yes, it was! _____ I'll do better next week _____

WEEK 50

*It's Happening! Things are starting to
add up and are falling into place for you.*

What I expect to have accomplished by the end of this week:

_____

_____

_____

_____

_____

Monday:_____

Tuesday: _____

Wednesday:_____

Thursday: _____

Friday: _____

What have you learned about yourself?_____

_____

What have you learned about what you are doing? _____

_____

Did you meet your goals and expectations? _____

_____

If your answer is yes, how so? If your answer is no, why not?

_____

Was your week an overall success? Check one.

Yes, it was! _____ I'll do better next week _____

WEEK 51

The plan is to reach your goals and be happy. Keep your happiness close to you.

What I expect to have accomplished by the end of this week:

_____

_____

_____

_____

_____

Monday:_____

Tuesday: _____

Wednesday:_____

Thursday: _____

Friday: _____

What have you learned about yourself?_____

_____

_____

What have you learned about what you are doing? _____

_____

_____

Did you meet your goals and expectations? _____

_____

_____

If your answer is yes, how so? If your answer is no, why not?

_____

_____

Was your week an overall success? Check one.

Yes, it was! _____ I'll do better next week _____

WEEK 52

You did it! Congratulations on being so amazing!
You put your mind to it and you made it happen·
There is no stopping you now· What's next?

What I expect to have accomplished by the end of this week:

_____
_____
_____
_____
_____

Monday:_____
Tuesday: _____
Wednesday:_____
Thursday: _____
Friday: _____
What have you learned about yourself?_____
_____
_____

What have you learned about what you are doing? _____
_____
_____

Did you meet your goals and expectations? _____
_____
_____

If your answer is yes, how so? If your answer is no, why not?
_____
_____

Was your week an overall success? Check one.
Yes, it was! _____ I'll do better next week _____

CPSIA information can be obtained
at www.ICGtesting.com
Printed in the USA
LVHW081919060921
697022LV00018B/313